MW01625012

Lilies for Looper

Rachel Foster Stuart
Illustrated by Mary Belcher

Kaleidoscope Books
I Am My Life™ Publishing, LLC
Durham, NC

Lilies for Looper
By Rachel Foster Stuart
Kaleidoscope Books (a children's book division of I Am My Life™ Publishing, LLC)
I Am My Life™ Publishing, LLC

Published by I Am My Life™ Publishing, LLC, Durham, NC

Manufactured in the United States of America.

Cover and Interior design: Yvonne Parks, Pear Creative, www.pearcreative.ca
Illustrator: Mary Belcher, www.marybelcher.com
Author's photograph: University of North Carolina at Chapel Hill, School of Social Work, Susan E. White
Illustrator's photograph: Mary Belcher, www.marybelcher.com

Publisher's Cataloging-In-Publication Data
(Prepared by The Donohue Group, Inc.)

Names: Stuart, Rachel Foster. | Belcher, Mary, illustrator.
Title: Lilies for Looper / Rachel Foster Stuart ; illustrated by: Mary Belcher.
Description: [Durham, North Carolina] : [Kaleidoscope Books, a children's book division of I Am My Life Publishing, LLC], [2017] | Interest age level: 4 and up. | Summary: One day six-year-old Looper and her parents head to a neighborhood fair after her team wins its softball game. There are many fascinating sights but Looper is drawn to a display of Stargazer lilies. After introducing herself to the flower seller, she immediately thrusts her face into the bouquet. Although the pollen covers her in gold dust, this experience is actually a happy accident, as it ends up revealing creative abilities she didn't know she had.
Identifiers: LCCN 2016960802 | ISBN 978-0-9973805-0-7 (paperback) | ISBN 0-9973805-0-0 (paperback) | ISBN 978-0-9973805-1-4 (hardcover) | ISBN 0-9973805-1-9 (hardcover) | ISBN 978-0-9973805-2-1 (ebook) | ISBN 0-9973805-2-7 (ebook)
Subjects: LCSH: Wonder in children--Juvenile fiction. | Errors--Juvenile fiction. | Lilies--Juvenile fiction. | Creative ability--Juvenile fiction. | CYAC: Wonder--Fiction. | Errors--Fiction. | Lilies--Fiction. | Creative ability--Fiction.
Classification: LCC PZ7.1.S78 Li 2017 (print) | LCC PZ7.1.S78 (ebook) | DDC [E]--dc23

The mission of I Am My Life™ Publishing, LLC: Integrous Proliferation of Human Good

For Mike

Looper loves flowers. She has since she was a little girl. Even though she is six years old now and still little, this has been her passion for as long as she can remember.

Her mom and dad take her to farmers' markets, botanical gardens, and greenhouses in between their everyday commitments and chores.

One day, after Looper's softball game, the team celebrated their victory by going to the town square. They saw many beautiful and inviting sights, such as a clown blowing up balloons into the shape of hearts, potters making bowls out of clay, and weavers spinning lovely rugs out of yarn.

MS. MacKinac's MAGICAL BLOOMS
FRESH FRUIT
ATTY'S POTTERY
WOVEN WORKS

Ms. MacKinac's
MAGICAL BLOOMS
HONEY
JAM
JAM

This is fun, Looper thought as she wandered from booth to booth, drinking in the excitement of people creating beautiful things for their friends to enjoy.

She skipped over to the area where farmers were selling their fresh homegrown tomatoes and basil, and she noticed some glorious flowers next to the woman selling coffee and cheese.

Hmm, what are these flowers? thought Looper as she quickly headed off in their direction.

"Hi there," Looper said to the woman selling the flowers. "My name is Looper, and these flowers are very pretty. What are they called?"

"Hi, Looper. My name is Miss Mackinac. These are Stargazer Lilies. Why don't you smell them?"

Looper immediately pushed her nose deep into the middle of the curly, shocking-pink petals dotted with maroon and took a deep breath. Her world filled up with the most delicious scent. It smelled like a mixture of fresh-baked cookies and licorice.

"Pretty special, huh?" Miss Mackinac asked Looper.

Just then, Looper's mom and dad came over. "There you are," they said in unison, laughing when they noticed that Looper's nose was covered in golden dust from the orangish-yellow flower stamens that shoot straight up.

"Looks like you put your nose in the honey jar, Loop," said Looper's dad.

Looper looked at herself in the mirror her mom held out before her and started to laugh.

She reached up, wiped some of the dust off her nose, and swiped her fingers across a piece of paper that Miss Mackinac used to record her flower sales. To her amazement, the golden dust made a perfect, gentle swirl across the piece of paper.

"Look! I can paint with flower dust!" Looper exclaimed as she quickly finger-painted a butterfly on the paper.

"My, but that is very beautiful!" Miss Mackinac nearly shouted as she marveled at the drawing before her.

"It looks like we'll have to set up a booth for you next week so that you can share your discovery with everybody," said Looper's dad. "We'll take a dozen lilies, Miss Mackinac. A dozen lilies for Looper."

FLOWERS
FOR
SALE

FLOWER
PAINTINGS
FOR
SALE

When Looper went to bed that night, she was thinking about her day and was so very happy in her heart. *Wow, I thought I made a mistake by getting lily dust on my nose and clothes, but as it turns out, it was a good accident*.

Soon after Looper had this thought, Looper's mom and dad came to tuck her in, and they saw that she was smiling. Looper was so pleased with herself.

"Honey, you thought getting flower dust on your nose was bad, but look at what you created," said Looper's mom as she pointed to the picture of the butterfly above Looper's bed. "This is the wonderment of life, Looper."

"Wonderment—what's that?" asked Looper.

"It's when you have respect and admiration for everything around you at all times," replied Looper's dad. "Even what seems bad in the moment may not be bad after all."

Looper wasn't exactly sure what her dad meant, but she held close the warmth she felt in her heart as she drifted off to sleep.

ABOUT THE AUTHOR

Rachel Foster Stuart was born and raised in Michigan. She has since lived in several other states while serving in the United States Air Force. She is a practicing clinical social worker who received a bachelor's degree from Central Michigan University. Rachel went on to receive her master's degree from Case Western Reserve University and then a doctorate from the University of North Carolina at Chapel Hill. Her published work mostly focuses on efforts to prevent family violence.

Rachel believes that promoting tolerance and understanding are core elements of living from the heart. She seeks to promote these values through her creative writing. As a Michigan native, Rachel draws on fond memories, themes, and places from her home state to create her characters and stories. *Lilies for Looper* is her first children's book.

Rachel currently lives in Washington, D.C. with her husband, Mike.

ABOUT THE ILLUSTRATOR

Mary is a long-time resident of Washington, D.C., who paints streetscapes and maps. Her watercolors are known for their strong colors and rich detail. She sells her work each weekend at Eastern Market on Capitol Hill.

Mary's work has been commissioned by the U.S. Forest Service Visitors Center, The Nature Conservancy, Blair House Restoration Fund, Reading Is Fundamental, D.C. Convention Center Authority, DAR Museum, Stephen Decatur House Museum, the White House Historical Association, National Building Museum, and many others. *Lilies for Looper* is the only children's book she has illustrated.

Mary studied photography at the Corcoran School of Art and later received a journalism degree from the University of Colorado at Boulder. As a newspaper reporter, she covered the White House, Capitol Hill and Justice Department. Before becoming a full-time artist in 1996, she was the spokesperson for Iran-Contra Independent Counsel Lawrence Walsh and was chief editor of his final report on the criminal investigations and trials.

Draw your favorite flower here!